MAKE LEGIT MONEY ONLINE WITH THESE 12
BUSINESS TYPES
WRITTEN BY DESIRE OLABISI OLAOSEGBA

First Published 2020

Published by

Desire Olabisi Olaosegba &

Kindle Direct Publishing, Amazon.

1996-2018, Amazon.com, Inc. or its affiliates. All Rights
Reserved. Amazon and Kindle are trademarks of
Amazon.com, Inc. or its affiliates. 410 Terry Avenue
North Seattle, Washington 98109 U.S.

ISBN: 9798-664-228-588

Printed by Kindle Direct Publishing, Washington.

DEDICATION

ACKNOWLEDGEMENT

With a heart of gratitude, I dedicate this Book to God Almighty for endowing me with an exceptional gift and granting me the opportunity to be ranked amongst the Published Authors of this World. Thank you Jesus for standing by me always.

To the glory of God, I hereby dedicate this Book to my Sweet Mother and my Beloved Son, Mrs A. Olaosegba and Master Oluwanifemi Bishop. Thank you for your inspirations from the beginning of this great Book till date. I am so grateful for the encouragement and believe you both had in me that I could become a Published Author and today, I am counted as one. Thank you so much Mummy and my Dearest Son for bearing with me, for all the sleepless nights I caused you while writing this Book.

I sincerely thank my beloved Daddy and my amiable Brothers for their support.

I specially send my immeasurable gratitude to my kind-hearted Uncle, Uncle Remi for his support towards this laudable achievement in my life.

I joyfully thank my very special friend for the encouragement and support always and also to the entire family of Olaosegba. I am really grateful to you all.

PREFACE

The current situation in the World has ushered in a new normal where there is a need to work remotely from home in order to keep safe and healthy. This new normal has been made easy with the help of technology. The Telecommunications sector also, is playing a vital role in the change we are experiencing now in the Business World.

INTRODUCTION

Online Businesses could be tricky, so you have to possess a clear and opened mind; as well as the right knowledge and tools to choose from a wide range of varieties that are legitimate in line with your lifestyle and aspirations. The Online Business that works for Mr. A may not work for Mr. B because of their different personal traits, interests and preferences.

Thus in this Book, I have carefully selected 12 different legitimate Online Businesses you can venture into and explore without any fraudulent activity attached to them.

At the end of this Book, readers should be able to know:

1. What an online business is
2. Types of online businesses in legal terms
3. What a legitimate online business means
4. What an illegitimate online business means
5. Legitimate online Business types available for you

TABLE OF CONTENTS

(i)   WHAT IS AN ONLINE BUSINESS?

An online business is simply defined as a business
carried out on the internet or web between two or more
people. An online Business has no physical business
meetings place but meetings between the sell and buyer
or prospective clients are done on the internet through
various technological tools and applications like: Zoom,
Skye, Cloud meetings, e-commerce stores interactions
and exchange, websites, Facebook, Google stores,
Instagram, Twitter etc.

In general, an online business involves the exchange of goods and services through the internet without any physical connection done. Mostly, a very successful business transaction done online sometimes extends to meeting physically for more transactions. This further leads to a stronger relationship between the seller and buyer.

While for some others, they mainly source for their prospective customers online and physically transact business with them because of the wide reach of people and millions of customers they can get access to online.

TYPES OF ONLINE BUSINESSES IN LEGAL TERMS

LEGITIMATE ONLINE BUSINESS

a. Legitimate Online Business is a business that is acceptable by law and made available for people to transact on without any fraudulent activity involved in it

b. ILLEGITIMATE ONLINE BUSINESS

is a business not acceptable by law and such a business is involved in fraudulent activities such as cybercrimes, stealing of monies, deceitful online business scams, etc.

MODULE TWO

THE 12 LEGITIMATE ONLINE BUSINESSESES

1. AN AFFILIATE.

To be an affiliate, you have to apply to become an affiliate with reputable companies or organizations you are interested in. Ensure you carryout research on the Company to be sure they don't undertake any fraudulent activity.

An Affiliate is a partner to the Organization working to ensure growth for the organization. In this kind of Business, you are required to promote a product and direct sales to that organization and get paid Commissions in percentage of what is actually bought through your sales link.

Here, you are meant to select the product or products of your choice and sell for the producer of the product both

in goods and in service delivery for a commission. Commission is usually calculated in percentage.

Sometimes in a big firm, an affiliate can receive up to $2,000 per sale which is subject to size of the company, turnover of the product, consumer satisfaction and profit level of that product. Some affiliate programmes/agent take less like $200 or 3-9% on product sold.

2. FREELANCER.

A Freelancer works as an entrepreneur, bargains on Online jobs given in the area of product sale or service without getting attached to the Company but only to render his/ her services on the required number of days and get paid the bargained amount.

Here, jobs are declared and bidded upon and each job declared goes to the best bidder. Payment is done at the completion of the job given. Sometimes, milestone payments are given in time. A Freelancer can collect jobs from different clients according to his/ her capacity but to be cautious not to disappoint any of his/ her clients in order not to loose them. A Freelancer can earn up to $100 to $2000 or more for jobs bided for.

You can be a Freelancer in the following areas: (a) Lead generation (b) Marketing/Sale (c) IT Installation (d) Website design (e) Digital marketing (f) Branding and many more

3. DIRECT SALES OF GOODS ON E-COMMERCE STORES AND THE VARIOUS SOCIAL MEDIA E.g. GOOGLEPLUS, FACEBOOK, PINTEREST, INSTAGRAM, TWITTER, TUMBLR AND OTHERS.

This entails placing your items for sale on e-commerce stores like Amazon, Shopify, Konga, Jumai. and others. You are required to pay commission in percentage for selling your products. This enables your product or service to reach millions of people all over the world by renting a space for your store for a particular fee. It's renewable and make sure your items are well packaged and attractive with reasonable price tag.

To succeed in the various e-commerce platform, for example, Amazon, you must make sure you maintain great products reviews and seller ratings and manage inventory, fulfil and ship Amazon orders.

Selling on other social media platforms too can be greatly enterprising when you are good at what you are offering to the your clients or prospective customers. As a social media marketer, firstly, you must have enough fans, followers, followings, subscribers that you would market your products to online. Secondly, you must be ready to run promotions for your products or services adverts to convince your prospective customers and the last but not the least step is that , you must know your target market and ensure that your products get to your exact target market which in turn assures sales positivity.

As a direct sale, you handle the packing, customs, shipping of the order of your products.

4. INDIRECT SALE OF GOODS

Here, you can place your items online with Amazon
market place and other e-commerce stores like Shopify
for them to help sell your products, handle payments,
take care of orders, customs, packing, shipment.

You will be paid for goods sold after all the agreed
charges are deducted for selling for you.

5. CREATING YOUR OWN WEBSITE

Website opens up an avenue for you to make recurring
income by monetizing your website with sale of

products, subscriptions, donations, fees, trainings
and content sales.

You can easily advertise your products on your site also
and make direct sales to your Customers and Clients.
You can place adverts for people for an agreed amount.
On your website, people can subscribe to paid
Newsletters or Journals, shop online through your
website which leads to additional income from affiliate
marketing.

6. ONLINE CONSULTANT.

There are so many services you can render to
your clients online according to your area of
specialization. A fee for the services rendered is
charged by you. There are a wide range of
Consultancy Services online for you to select
from but you must be well qualified and certified
to carryout such services. Some Online
Consultancy Services include:

(a) Resources, Outsourcing Services

(b) Financial advisor/ Counsellor

(c) Legal advisory consulting

(d) Career guidance and Counselling Services

(e) Marriage counselling services

(f) Business growth Consultancy

For each different consultancy role, the Consultant must possess an approved qualification and certification from relevant bodies.

7. SHORT SCRIPT WRITER

Writing of short scripts for publishers can make you earn from $100-$300 per day. Your short stories could be based on your area of interest in sports, education, story telling, adventure, business etc.

8. CONTENT CREATOR ON YOUTUBE

Here, you need to have a Channel on YouTube showcasing your area of expertise and reaching millions of people in the world which in turn helps to grow your brand leading to more views and profit taking.

Ensure your content on YouTube is of great value to your viewers and subscribers.

Kids and teenagers can create contents that are educational and that would build them morally to become the leaders of tomorrow E.g. Educational books, story books, poems, short plays, talent shows etc.

Worlds Extraordinary Kids | Talent Genius Kids - YouTu

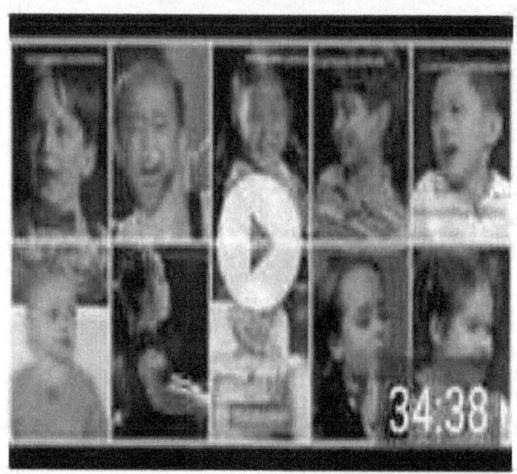

---

9. TYPIST- BEGINNER, INTERMEDIATE AND EXPERT LEVELS

As a Typist, you can earn huge online by typing the following:

(a) manuscript (b) resume (c) project research work.

Typists are graded into three different levels: the beginners level, the intermediate level and the experience expert level.

Rate of payment also are being calculated hourly according to the level of the Typist and delivery of work done at a stipulated date and time. TYPIST are paid

hourly and are paid in dollars

10. ONLINE TUTOR You can generate applicants ready for exams and tutor them online. Also, private lessons on particular subjects that seems difficult for a group of students can be taught online using tools like:

Zoom and Skye depending on the number of students you are tutoring at that point in time and you will be paid hourly in dollars. You could tutor other short courses online, webinars etc.

As a Tutor, you could also be a live COACH for your team players, young football, basketball, volleyball teams by tutoring them online. Likewise, a gym coach training his or her clients on the daily exercising tips for a healthy living.

11. PROOF READER OR AN EDITOR

As a Proof Reader, you are engaged with reading through the copy of the manuscript or letter checking for errors like misspellings, typographical errors, wrong use of punctuation marks.

A Proof reader works directly with a Publishing firm and other companies alike with the need for an error free grammatical report to be presented to the public or those in need of such information.

A Proof reader earns a minimum of $50 or more per day. To become an Editor, you would go a step further by checking the grammatical arrangement of the manuscript. Ensuring there is no error in the grammatical arrangement of the report or manuscript. The Editor's duty is to bring clarity to the write up and this can lead to a change in the tone and improve the readability of the manuscript.

An Editor earns more than a Proof reader because he/she ensures the report or manuscript is good enough to be published and must possess the right qualifications to carryout his/her duties.

12. RESEARCH SURVEYS

You can carryout surveys for various researchers or clients in need of it and be paid handsomely. You can carryout the surveys in the following areas:

(a) Product Launch Survey.

(b) Business Survey- Business Strategy.

(c) Sales Survey

(d) Consumer satisfaction survey (e) Research jobs on

Education. (f) Research on the Economy

(g) Scientific Research

h) Research jobs on new discoveries

(i) Research jobs on Technology

(j) Survey of employees satisfaction

Online Researchers are paid well for promptly carrying out their duties effectively and efficiently.

CONCLUSION

In conclusion, making legitimate earnings online is truly made easy with this expository e-book. The sole decision lies in you to make your preferred choice of online business and start earning right away.

Do you agree?

Kindly write your comments or suggestions in the review session of this e-book on Amazon.

Thanks.

MAKE LEGIT MONEY ONLINE

DESIRE OLABISI

WITH THESE 12 BUSINESS TYPES

www.ingramcontent.com/pod-product-compliance
Lightning Source LLC
Chambersburg PA
CBHW030554220526
45463CB00007B/3081